YES AND I

William Seamwell

7 : xi : 80

Yes And No

WILLIAM SCAMMELL

HARRY CHAMBERS/PETERLOO POETS

First published in 1979
by Harry Chambers/Peterloo Poets
Treovis Farm Cottage, Upton Cross, Liskeard, Cornwall PL14 5BQ

ISBN 0 905291 18 2

Printed in Great Britain by
Latimer Trend & Company Ltd Plymouth

ACKNOWLEDGEMENTS are due to the editors of *Bananas, Critical Quarterly, London Magazine, New Poetry, Outposts, P.E.N. Broadsheet, Poetry* (Chicago), *Poetry Review, Raven* and *Transatlantic Review*, in whose pages some of these poems first appeared.

'Robert Lowell' first appeared in *New Poetry 4* (Arts Council, 1978).

Cover Painting: PIERO di COSIMO, Profile of a Young Woman (Musée Condé, Chantilly).

Harry Chambers/Peterloo Poets receives financial assistance from The Arts Council of Great Britain

For J

Contents

Somewhere To Live

Another small town. This one has a castle,
a brewery hard by, and two strong rivers
that shake the earth like newspaper presses in a basement.

The park is high on a sugarloaf hill.
At dusk mist rises from the town's spine
like great whiffs of piety from a medieval manuscript

and smoke brushes oriental beauties on the sky.
There's a fountain dedicated to Wordsworth
with a Mabel Lucy Attwell child on top

turning her back on sombre fells.
From up here All Saints looks like
a ship stuck fast in the builder's yard.

Market days, sheep and cattle jam the steel pens
in the auctioneer's yard. After the singsong
the concrete is hosed of its urine and shit.

The people are broad, tough, convivial
after their fashion. Youth has learnt vandalism,
dursn't tangle though with the unimported world

of sheep, cows, tractors, rock.
Once a year they race down the rapids
in frail canoes. Everyone gets a prize.

The railway station's been demolished.
Roads squiggle unromanly off
in their own looping vernacular

and the daily news is rain—rain
the size of washing-up bowls, ferocious
as the leaping rock that marries it

every dropped yard of the way.

9

St. Bees In Winter

The kids shoot out of the car roaring
to meet their maker—instantly attuned
to that huge battery and assault. High tide,
high winds, shriek at the gaping shore;
they shriek right back, like pebbles
flung back and forth in the sling of surf.
One picks at daisy chains of foam;
the next is hooting back the ebb; then all,
mad as bullfighters, are down the sea's mouth,
dwarfed by the breakers' thundering rush.
Wet feet, wet legs, wet bouncing bottoms . . .
I swear if we loosed the rein of our eyes
they'd be out of this world in minutes,
tumbled through to the sinners and saints
gunning their ghostly spray at our white lips.

'Queen Mary'

'What time does this place get to New York?'
Bea Lillie is supposed to have said.
And true it was the size of a walled town—
old York, perhaps—with guilds of stewards,
waiters, barmen; a ruling caste of officer
barons; and a long-running morality play
called the sea. Dicky Davis announced
bingo numbers then, in training for TV.
The ship wore the robes of empire, tasteless
but undeniably grand. Orson Welles stumped
Promenade Deck like Wolfit playing Lear.

But when we hit the Atlantic, a blazing
rig of light and towered steel, she
was just another ship, though with her own
unique and shuddering movement. I suppose
it took half a hundred planetary waves
to throw her slowly up on end. She poised
in mid-air a moment, then slowly slowly
sank, curtseying to the gods: hit bottom
with a great shuddering crash as though fallen
on her ass: and shook groaning there for
hours, abased and suicidal. Then up and up
and up, still in slow motion like a dream,
as grossly presumptuous now as previously
tearing at her breast—a monstrous Fool
aping the manners at court. Bad days
she'd roll at the same time. Immigrants
groaned in Tourist; strong Englishmen
clenched their pipes in Cabin; old Hollywood
took curtain calls up in the Silver Grille—
Crepe suzettes, Dom Perignon, and technicoloured
tuxedos, their sturdy wives' décolletage
as startling as the waves. I perched
in a fetid darkroom in the bows, conjuring
their likenesses from reeking chemicals
and retching fit to bust, while Leviathan

11

bulldozed running walls of green and white
shrieking on through her quotidian bedlam
till Wall Street's answering octaves cried us home.

Now, sold and burnt, gutted like a fish
the old lady gasps rotting somewhere
on America's west and crankiest coast,
recalcitrant still, a colony of rust
stooped and livid, robed in that slow fire.

Except The Dying

'The last night that she lived
It was a common night
Except the dying; this to us
Made nature different'
—*Emily Dickinson*

I remember a woman with long Alice hair
pale delicate limbs, and large-minded skills
whose legs took her walking surprisingly far
by day and by night in the Gloucestershire hills.
    She loved books and parties
       and dancing and talk
    but the life she was planning
       was never rebuilt.

She went up to Oxford from school, where she met
and mated a minor young aristocrat.
    He wrote and he printed
       from his large reserves
    a waste-landish view of
       the state of his nerves.
Soon she was pregnant, and rounded with life
apprenticed and trading as mother and wife.

He gave her three children, then slowly dropped out
drifting abroad into fashionable ills:
drugs, homosexuals, communal young touts
flown back and shown off in the Gloucestershire hills.
    In a picturesque cottage
       with only a view
    she tended the tidings
       of love's residue.

One mad day in summer, pride-galled beyond fear
he razored his throat in a roomful of friends.
She flew off to Spain to collect all the gear—
car, papers, typewriter, the odds and the ends
of a life that had sharpened
and tempered her own,
husbanded now by
equivocal stone.

She worked hard, investing the money she'd free;
brought up the children; resumed her career,
studying part-time for a proper degree
and falling in love with another young seer.
He wrote too, and drank
a most clubbable villain
not born to be Hamlet
but our village Dylan.

They argued and shouted, fought out epic fights
tearing the rind from all daily delights:
ending it, starting it, minds at full charge—
just like an ordinary marriage writ large.
She loved books and parties
and dancing and bed
and larger-than-life men
who did what she said.

For her eyes could be stony, her voice rather shrill;
her fine mind was matched by the strength of her will.
She knew about men as she knew about gods—
a childish collection of sceptical sods
powered by self-love
and grandiose texts,
erratically fuelled
by theories and sex.

The wheel came full circle: she pedalled off back
to Oxford to doctor her mind to the full,
the writer established, the ménage intact,
the children quite brilliantly finishing school.
Back to the common room's
yellow and bronze
quads full of autumn
and clever young dons.

But beginnings were all that she savoured; for now
a cancerous growth feathered life in mid-breath:
one minute she quivered, full-stretched as a bow
then brutely unstrung and flung early to death.
We watched at the service;
no comfort was there
in the vicar's right readings
or yew-enclosed air.

Last, common law husband and children walked high
up on Bellbarrow Hill, where they scattered the ash
as she'd wanted, the stones of an old fort nearby
soundlessly slipping down into the grass.
Thus ended the parties
the marvellous self-will.
Like Alice, she's scampered
back into the hill.

Spring Song

Of all the symphonies, *Jupiter* wears best.
A kitten abseils down the wicker chair.
This whisky augurs well. After tennis
my wife glows in the dusk like earthenware.

When mildly drunk, Richard Strauss will do—
Four Last Songs to polychrome the head.
Sex and death forever! One fits like a shoe,
the other, barefoot, amorously tiptoes
                              to
                                    my
                                          bed

                    envoi
Pyramids, long barrows, tumps and tombs,
urns, sepulchres, mounds, marble vaults,
all granite of all graves, all women's wombs
reach backwards, pocketing time's faults;

spend all we have to give, unloose the dust
that packed itself into a little ball
and bounced us here to love. Dearest, we must
love to our destruction, or not love at all.

Beginnings

Immoveable yet moving, their sirens blasting
a last trump to stir the solid dead
huge liners wormed down the estuary
and crashed softly through world's end.

Under returning eyes, the wash slapped
at the beach. Twice every day the tidal door
swung back, baring its larder of rank smells.
A few fishermen dug bait; gulls drilled

below the wrack; the pier stood trussed and naked,
going nowhere. In muddy creeks we learnt to swim
spitting hard salt water from our lungs,
white and skinny as the dry pointed sedge.

A swath of open heath rolled to old woods
where ponies flicked drifting in brown shoals,
stubborn, shy, compounding with the scent
all dumbly chased. Bright winter

hands clutched frozen trophies, pawned
later at painful fires; or dockhead horns
pumped out a ground bass at the fog
which scarfed each echo, robed us in its cry.

*   *   *

The village ticked on solid and monotonous,
an old clock that under the hammer now
fetches huge capricious prices.
Not a field or a copse but dropped

to the developers swarming JCBs.
I live in the country still, where farmers
plot and spit; their sullen acres
mass along the ridge. On market days

our minds inspect their license. Way back
we circled the green patch of things, targets
for our shooting. It stood there, stiff,
hieratic, and blew our silly brains out.

Death Of Auden

Yes he was deeply unhappy
and will live as before with regret.
Queerly prescient his words will continue
to race round the track and be met

by these who also watch truth
white-coated on the tracks of skill:
one red hand holds the leash
the other the mercy-killer that kills.

Was he a great writer? Heigh
and ho: this way to the museyroom.
The world's unjust, let's merely say,
if he's not in a limestone catacomb

housekeepered by Miss Gee in tights
valeted by friendly dons
Mozart from the stalactites
runic sermons round his bones.

Today in the middle of a dripping wood
the hush of pines held solid dark
as tangible a livelihood
as sunlight in a summer park.

Fanny To Charles Kingsley

'We will undress and bathe and then you will come
to my room, and we will kiss and love very much
and read psalms aloud together, and then we will
kneel down and pray in our nightdresses. Oh! what
solemn bliss! How hallowing! And then you will take me up
in your arms, will you not? And lay me down in bed. And
then you will extinguish our light and come to me!
How I will open my arms to you and then sink
into yours! And you will kiss me and clasp me
and we will both praise God alone in the dark night
with His eyes shining down upon us and His love
enclosing us. After a time we shall sleep . . .'

The world's rude eyes are propped open, Fanny,
by your exclamation marks. Posterity's programmed
lips invite you to an analytic kiss, couched in
unloving certainty. Bedrooms now are for bodies only,
multiplied by mirrors. Love on, praise the Lord and his works
without whining. Our bliss is neither solemn nor shining.

Remembering The Great War

Opaque and resonant as sacred texts
the names alone sound out a litany:
Passchendaele, Ypres, the Somme, Verdun . . .

Some dropped perfect but for a sweet
smudge of gas—others, dispersing, spanned
earth in the wildest hug.

Men flashed hissing to their elements
like spit gobbed on a stove. One officer
in nomansland apologised to his troops

behind for lasting in such loud slow screams.
Four men unwound their lives to staunch
his uproar—failed, like the concerted knuckles

hammered round his teeth. Gowned neutrally
for christenings, deaths, history thumbs
its cheap editions, weltering in echoes.

I think of Sassoon's tall heart, contracting
fiercest love for his own men, one of whom
shot him from excess of zeal; of Graves's

stretched contempts. The fires they grazed rot down
in village squares. On memory's floor words rut
and root, nosing blind and ghastly at the tongue.

Heatwave

All Latins now, slipping into neutral,
letting the tongue wag on.
The body is supremo. Armies
of them swagger the shops and streets,
each promoted general, passing out
at the universal peace parade.
The sun's turned pandar, spooning
out flesh in banks and offices;
to think is tantamount
to buttoning on a trade gap.
Look! the men are modest
as a Yorkshire opening bat;
and these advancing hips
have scissored all the headlines to confetti.

Sons And Lovers

Of all schools, commend me to the Stoicks
Walter Scott, *Journals*

Full on the lips, eyes serious and wide,
arms scooping me out of the adult mist
my son bestows affection like a fist
unleashing love. His schoolboy pride
yells 'Red alert!' and jerks eyes shut
when on the screen some sultry slut

distracts the cowboy with a showdown kiss,
but that other switched-on world of violence
seems not to impinge on this one—hence
the congruous bedtime ritual. This
wife of mine, and mother too, throw the same
uncanny, unsophisticated flame

of explicit, daylight love; whereas I
avert laconic eyes and spur my snorting horse
towards some distant ranch, from which to curse
and spy out hunters of the heart, and sigh
as my badman cards withhold the wanted ace:
always, between them and me, some neutral space.

I can cope with the slut, hourglass of breasts
and hips. It's the lifelong walk down mainstreet,
the talk and level expectations straight
from the barrel of a daily need that tests
me to destruction: bright hooves of love
racing me off to justice and the hangman's shove.

Night Piece

The latest Dylan warbles from the speakers
on kissing terms with poetry and kitsch;
descendant of those popular lay preachers
lamenting Adam's mating with a bitch.

The winged armchair has flown the wife's dear head
into a needed sleep, Colette's pert pages
abandoned on her lap. We've talked and said
enough to wear away the rock of ages.

The children burrow calmly on through school
and home and our eternal remonstrations,
diviners of true feeling, visceral
as third-world members of united nations.

I joint up books and plays for impulse buyers,
blotched hands down among the intestines;
you orchestrate our rhythms, light the fires,
process the dirty washing through machines.

On taut strung lines of disregarded days
we flap and fly, revolve like bleached-out shirts,
our daily acts a sort of paraphrase
of all the ancient texts and modern hurts.

But now the whole house sleeps; the firelight gleams;
the evening shapes itself into a bowl
which holds us still and precious, while our dreams
confront the buried core, or Dylan's howl.

A.G.M.

Grey bomber clouds
hover in tight
formation; mad
Zephyrus licks
frozen chops; now
for the crunch,
the eight-month
mastication till
the puny burp
of spring, hot air
conducting a few
million sperm
to their short
spawn. O children
of the north
duck to your holes:
the chairman
is to declare
his dividends.

Light's ill, fades
to a terminal grey;
amphibious cars
hiss by; hobbies
are resurrected,
meals lengthened,
fires read like
living entrails.
A hothouse rhythm
at the disco,
transplants up at
the old folks home.
Here in my house
distant now
from obvious needs

the bow hangs slack
in the hall
and we are stalked
by what we mocked.
Trees strip for
the amorous snow—
all lovers
adore pain—
the hedgehog
draws credits
on a balance
he never doubted
and we who once
tipped the scales
now dust the floor
of the shop like
chaff. Blubbering
into convenience foods
we fist aspirin
or home-brew,
swallow just so
much of the void
as will hollow
a cheque book or
fuel our dream
thermals. One home
and two aways
might stick us
in the jam.

Keith Douglas

Levelled the big gun of words
at names of war and women

tight-lipped as a scar
that whitens yearly in the skin;

and learned how cleverness must
against itself enlist.

How combative the poets!
Tracked iambs shoot it out

with tradition and a real-life
enemy served up like a meal

to a hungry man. He choked
on war's nutritions, as others

on what symbols they can muster.
Now they are all sated,

healed, dropped from themselves
like a scab that's eloquent

of something done
and sealed up in the doing.

Their premises concluded
words mark them, stone on stone.

Aunt Jenny

Propped up on pillows
like a sharp effigy of pain
she hollowed out
the hours of many nights,

memory telling its fortune,
lungs clutching air.
She played duets with a young man
cancelled out in France,

flung away like a used ticket
in the gentry's big concert.
Rammed corks between
tiny fingers to span an octave,

adding articulate sound
to the struck attitudes
on the silent screen
while studying for

the concert career
that never came. She had
asthma, laboured to draw breath.
Two decades dealt out

a husband, Depression, another
war. Their only child died
before reaching one.
I remember them

smiling out of snapshots
tin-helmeted against the blitz,
wardens of miles
of literal London rubble.

For the coronation Aunt Jenny
wore three cardigans,
sealed every door and window
before we hunched reverentially

over their tiny TV
and its perspex magnifier,
surrounded by flasks and sandwiches
for the unrepeatable marathon.

She perched on chairs
as on a ledge
from which she might fall
to breathlessness.

The flat, incendiary years
tilt and upend her
past all scrabbling.
Clothes to be sorted,

pillows smoothed
of her seismic impress.
I—fashions changing—
wear her old fur coat;

mortgage my pen
to dumb and useless fury.
Such shabby gods don't need
a very grand inquisitor.

Abandoned In Leicester

I've listened to learned papers on
the imagery of Tennyson
and now my fellow conferees
have gone to look at Somersby's
most famous son's still private mansion,
conducted thither by his grandson—

born in eighteen-seventy-nine
of that melancholy line
but looking now as if he'd rather
run a mile than be like grandfather:
spontaneous and sprightly as
Bob Cratchit's smile, or natural gas.

Lonely, doubting, full of pity,
my soul sinks in this strange city.
Shall I walk? Or sit and read?
Write a letter? Try the Beeb's
canned comfort for the traveller?
If I believed in the Hereafter

I'd get down on my knees and pray;
hypothesise it all away
amongst my spiritual reckonings.
Analysis, however, brings
no peace or grace to those like me
whose reason tells them God can't be;

who settle for a stoic stance
but learn that time, or love, or chance
will jolt them to their knees just when,
safely in their singular den,
they feel the need to touch—and find
only shadows of the mind

in books, or music, bars and parties,
shallow intellectual hearties:
dehydrated travesties
declaiming Job and Ecclesiastes
but whose lives are calmly pointed
by Mammon's suited and annointed.

Driven out by my heart's frown
eventually I walk downtown
avoiding football fans, whose moves
are shadowed by police in droves,
and follow the Saturday sun to Leicester's
covered market, manned by jesters

knowledgeable in known techniques
and all the tongues that money speaks.
There I find my proper alms:
A German Requiem by Brahms
in stereo, cheap. For years and years
that's summoned up symbolic tears—

ever since, in Hampstead church,
where disaffected young men lurch
from faith to faith, I first heard
Brahms's overpowering word.
Apt, I know, that I should choose
a mediated form of news,

a mode of touch and speech requiring
just me, and a room, and a bit of wiring;
emotion filed and finished, neat
as polished steel round crippled feet.
I hope the garden that summoned Maud
wasn't a similar kind of fraud

with roses laid out all in a row
and turf too tidy, driven snow
never dirtying into slush
and a wild-eyed man whose heart was crushed
not by a lovely and damnable she
but simply by self's strong misery.

Robert Lowell

(*died September 1977*)

Your lines swim on, obsessive as the flash
and hook of the fisherman's cast;
parables blackballed in the club. You
founded a new one: talented screwballs
only need apply. The unexampled force
of the new breeds sin, remorse,
disciples in the garden.
           There is a vein
of murderous sentiment that taints
a new world's joy—the hoods of Disney
and Capone sleekly furred with candy-
coloured blood, reeking of love and power,
the fabled violence of America
tugging even at you.
           'All life's grandeur
is something with a girl in summer':
despair or affirmation? Patrician, gambler,
you fed on collocation, throwing
friends, lovers, eras endlessly together
like novels on a shelf.—Of course I only guess.
But talent guarded your foolhardiness.
Expressionist, you hugged it tight
and taught a generation how to write
after the blitzkrieg of the moderns, of whom
you, Beckett were the heirs. Avatars of gloom
your baroque wrangle with God grew from
a single root. What trinitarian wine
you relished as you spat! All the way down
to hell it ran: Milton, Melville, *Miltown*,
long sizzling declensions of the sublime
unprincipled lure of the harpies. Time's
one-way barb electrifies the soul; love, sin
once wrenched ashore, haul their bright colours in,
fade to a name or genus. Husband, poet
consorting with the dead, their living hurt.

Above Thirlmere

Every lake has its sunken cathedral
where gilled monks do their offices
and tell the glassy hours. Their services
are watched by lonely teenagers, by owls

and couples growing old in cars. Who prays
for what is seldom known. Ribboning down
tall aisles young bridal rivers drown
their glances in the hush, the dying days

drift, stain the water's gift with echoes of
old jokes, old knowingness. These hooded learnt
so much that they have drowned, shocked into love's

alert and lidless eye. The water burns
to no hungry sea, no god enfolds
or casts his seine at nightfall.—Marriage terms.

The Barrows, Glasgow

The welfare state might never have been
nor needed either. A circus gaiety
pervades the streets crowded poverty,
every face stamped clear and clean
with unadjusted meanings. Manners
are medieval, transactions banners

of gothic humour and whisky-sodden
breath. Mile upon mile of bric-
a-brac and desirable junk, chaotic
as the municipal midden
or the inside of Coleridge's head,
and about as healthy. Here the dead

and dying fashions recombine—
fur coats, chinoiserie, old books,
King George saluting, pentateuchs
and bibles by the score, stripped pine
and dirty roll-top desks, pots and vases
to furnish flowers for a thousand ages.

Neither gales nor rain affect the mart.
The Kasbah seethes on like a city
undreamt by any planner, and we
who came here for a poker depart
with tureens and china sufficiently large
for Desperate Dan's or King George's ménage.

Two cheers for a noggin of the cold north!
where whisky and old fashions
inflate and explode the euphemisms.
The market grasps what things are worth
when handed down, as all things are,
unstatused, stalled at this bazaar.

High Lorton

Force-fed with rain and wind, the hanging fells
plump like an orange in the sun. Small sails
of grass draw down young skittering sheep. The larger
becks paw at root and rockface, stalk the nearest river.
A path winds up beneath funereal pines
whose branches nail down all the winds
and takes you to a drop: there in a space
populous with unlikely trees
bolt upright on tall rock, or clawing
at the cliff, lush weeds, strange groupings
and grotesques of stone and wood stand gaping
at the Force, that leaps the sopping air
as though all pleasure lay in waiting there
and sheers down to a pool, then, darkening, spills
on down the slope. The heart dies with that fall;
eyes rush to the bone-white edge, play back
the epic instant when, arching rock,
the long ecstatic plumes fan out and fall
plucking the sunlight with them. Rich, rank
and gloomy, the operatic falls bank
fresh deposits hourly, spent in the blink
of an eyelid. A green vaulted chasm
shifts all the mysteries of this orgasm
down to the lakes, which on a clear day show
the tops mutely trembling. They do it slow.

Nature Reserve

I saw a swan. It dibbled in the lake
like a comedian gargling with his lips
and after this food for thought slid
its unsmiling head straight to the bottom,
coming up with a small dark frog.
Two legs were trapped, the rest flopped
loosely down and out. Raising it high
from home the beak experimentally
fractioned apart to get a better grip
or aim, at which the frog snapped
half a leap, like a wet blowy sock
from a peg. But the beak snapped back
and the frog stood—hung—where it was,
while the seamless neck racked slowly
right and left. For some appalling time
he juggled the thing, like someone cramming
a lid on a drowning cat, or trying to stuff
elastic in a jar; and the frog danced hard;
but by degrees the jaws worked under
the body weight, and the balled will
slowed, centred high and lonely over the bone.
All up. The maw gulped sky and out
of the air dropped the frog, convulsing
to the python neck's long swallow.
He dibbled once again, as who should
dainty in a finger bowl, and setting his prow
up high paddled straight at me, for crumbs.

Riposte

The whining lover, that does place
His wonder in a painted face,
And wastes his substance in the chase,

Could not in melancholy pine,
Had he affections so divine,
As once to fall in love with wine.
—Charles Cotton, *Ode*

Pish! sir. Tosh! sir. Only a fool
Resigns a throne for a milking stool.
Love is inexhaustible.

Wine's a foolish substitute
For *Aphrodite*'s golden loot.
An ill-bred, vegetable suit

Like *Jason*'s never prospers, since
The only fleece that suits a prince
Is one that maids coyly evince.

To elevate drink above a girl
Is surely the most damnable
Of abdications. A brandy bowl

's a cold and sterile globe of glass
Appropriate to that dull ass
Consigned to *Onan*'s singleness.

Such brutish joys are counterfeits.
In this round world there's nothing fits
The hands quite like a pair of tits

That occupy their global place
In softly-saturated space
With utter tactile peace and grace.

They're *Chloe*'s—female paradigm
Of all that's earthy and divine.
And is, occasionally, mine!

She knows her worth, is not averse
In a largely sexual universe
To fingered warmth—time's knowing nurse

That breeds us stiffly up to feel
An age-old itch beyond repeal
To penetrate the really real.

I'd sooner gaze at a woman's eyes
Than drunkenly anatomise
The politicians' latest lies;

I'd rather pass, in subtleness
Of sweet discourse, the gentleness
Of evèning's discursiveness

With women's voices, soft and low,
Than muddled, gross and tiresome grow
With masculine fellatio.

(A somewhat desp'rate figure of speech
To indicate mouthfuls that teach
Us things beyond our single reach.)

I'd give up all the wine in *France*
For a biddable girl in flimsy pants.
Scotch for the *Scots*! so I advance

Sensuously towards my fall.
Even versing begins to pall
Beside that pelvic madrigal

Danced with consummate nonchalance
By nubile mothers, daughers, aunts,
Beneath their staid habiliments.

Is this wicked? Is it only me,
Humbert, and other such company
Are bound in perpetuity

To a flashing eye and a flesh-packed dress,
Sorcerer's apprentices
Hungry for *Nature*'s pointfulness?

Ah well! Ah well! Or win or lose
You, *Sir Charles*, sup up your booze
While I peruse the female news

And see what's doing in the stews
Where all our inclinations fuse,
Expiring in the final *Muse*.

Elements Of Learning

The wind
shakes Cumberland in its teeth
day after senseless day, as though in grief
at the heresy of objects.

Is it the ghost
of Heraclitus single-handedly proving
all things must move and keep on moving,
driving his logic

to a distant market?
Or some spirit leviathan
loosely confounding materialism?
Either way

I admire and loathe
it. My rooting mind has grown
as yellow-rotten as the grass beneath a stone
or some dazed

patient's drugged
and stinking breath. No doubt the wind
knows best but, thinner-skinned,
it might know better.

Convenor of pomp
and single-bloody-minded circumstance!
A mad shop steward ignorant
as a syllogism

nailing its thesis
to the door. Religion was ever thus,
herding the hills, raising a fuss,
demanding more.

Small wonder
the monks made gardens, imposed a season
of walled and shrubberied walks, sweet reason
thumbing its nose

at conviction's
swagger and club. Mind rounds on the pedagogue
as lambing sheep turn on the dog,
or grass splits stone.

Thousand And One Nights

Sitting in a bar in Kendal
as the rain washed another day
into the waiting gutters
I heard the jukebox say

'Baby everything is all right!
Baby everything's just fine!'
in one of those expressive voices
Americans often own

that shape the most lacklustre words
into surprising life,
as wind will sculpt a desert
or sandstone whet a knife.

I thought of all those poems
where conjunction is allegorised,
fixing a man and a moment
in resonant octaves of surmise:

and wondered what the jukebox
might have to say to that
as it flung its saws and sayings
at my retreating back.

Systematic Disclosures

'To be is to be the value of a variable'—Quine

Out of the mouths
of babes and logicians come worlds we know and live in.
The incidentals say so much more than the doctrine.

I don't suppose
Leibniz thought to father Pangloss, or Kant either
laboured to see 'thou best philosopher'

hung round
some child's unnecessary neck. Hardy's glooms, his teachings,
compel less whole assent than his wayside meetings:

Yeats's visions
and gyres than his patient isolation of the spirochetes
of age and failure—furies who met their Madame Curie.

Hence the familiar
paradox: felt truth will flower till the milky way
spills to oblivion, whereas profundities from the assembly bay

of necessary
revolutions fall always to rust and the academic re-toolers,
the cutters and trimmers and many-skilled jewellers.

These are the
unsorted variables we predicate life
and consciousness on, rusks that resist the knife

and fork
of two-valued logics, for we grub up choler with our clear soup
and many elastic attitudes keep in place our romper suit.

Once more with
mixed feeling: particulars are bought and paid for, theories rentals;
the doctrines tell us less than the incidentals.

High Summer

Heat pours from a pluperfect sky, sets
into a perfect summer's day.
Take off your shyness, clothes, regrets,

immerse yourself in water, bake lightly
brown on these hot stones and eat yourself
up, slowly. Then eat these motley

gorgeous girls who hop and preen
all over the beach. Backs bladed,
throats fluting men

to the priesthood or the poles; thighs
a million tides never quite reached.
O Christ! Buridan's ass might die

of data here: all move to the un-
Platonic eye of the sun,
prostrate with sensation.

In pubs, at evening, they've all risen
bare-shouldered, perfumed,
sipping at glasses like flowers.

Hot night brushes each eye and cheek.
Speech is continually stubbed out,
re-lit, discarded. Now see the velvet

of the mind smoothed the wrong way
as wind will darken water,
lightly drown the shallow light of day.

Late And Soon

There's something in the English air
that nourishes a cute despair.
All those poems about John Clare!

Regret drips from our pens like rain.
No screams, just muted sighs. Amen
behind the privet hedge. Amen . . .

Country Dance

Thou madest them wise to know
And wiser to ignore

—Wilfred Scawen Blunt

What do bodies mean, beyond pain
and excitement? Is it the heart
lifts legs or the mind's nimble flute?

The floor comes up and hits you, expansive, mute.

More Weather

Highjacked by wind, the day whirls off
into endless commotion. Neither love nor money
will ransome it, nor all the flying squads of trees

pin it back down on its foundations.
Stripped of their tin-foil peace
the lakes look more like the Channel on a bad day,

the lakelight atomised to driven spray.
Even the Dowager Windermere slops
into the road, kicking up her heels

as though reckless with the lunchtime martinis;
and every river from Cocker to Kent
is a boiling muddy brown reminder

that we might need to salvage more than hats.
No use trying to think or work or even
ponder that disjunction. The leaves are enjoying

a second life, utterly manic now and macabre:
mad bad children mocking their parents
and all the possible futures.

The sun beams down in cathedral shafts
from stained and hurrying clouds, then's
promptly slammed back over the horizon.

Today will not land until at least tomorrow,
probably in that far-off country of TV news
standing mysterious and vulnerable on the tarmac

wondering whether it used or was used by
any known thrust on the statutory books
of science or good intentions. Not

all gales blow themselves out.

Them

Kinder and saner
their lives branch out
like a leafy tree
to house whole cities
of domestic life,
whereas men either
ramble nowhere like a bush
or build themselves
into fortresses of prickly
authority, bending back
their importances to the best
and most fearsome advantage.

Truer and straighter
their shapely bodies
and riddling minds
tutor all principles
in particularity,
ground right and wrong
in the highest expediencies:
kin to the fragrant soil
that kicks up the dog's hind leg
to found a dynasty.
Their deductions never amount to less.

Finer and wiser
they lack arrogance
to amass fortunes
and pedantry to plait
a fugue or spit out wine
and dullness to sit in clubs
or colleges. Instead they knit
up families, write Christmas cards
to remote uncles, worry over tones
of voice and nameless diseases

and irresponsible fathers
and dull husbandly lovers;
slip in and out of modesty
like a pinafore.

Yes And No

All is from antithesis
　　—Yeats

Born within seconds of each other
and difficult to tell apart.

(The afterbirth flared like a sunspot,
dusting the pathologist's hands with ash.)

Nourished on the selfsame breasts
they fought for real, like logicians.

She liked snakes and horses,
he was good at inventing names.

Both kept late nights, declined
to join a political party or forward good causes.

He was slung out of Oxford,
Cambridge reported her unbalanced.

Close friends suspected them of incest.
Whatever you thought they'd already mapped it and moved on.

For a time they made a living as writers
but the reviewers saw no thematic growth.

Eventually and to no-one's surprise
she was discovered pregnant. Twins

would you believe? Disowned, of course,
and dropped in the lap of the state

which to this day levies taxes
on the transmission of thought.

Their end's not known. Various garden cities
reported some interminable wake.

Natural History

The gulls wheel in, repelling local crows,
then settle on the house ridge opposite.
Their quarrel never ceases, even amongst themselves.
Head battened down, beak bayonet fixed,
eyes popping at the young, one tanks along
red tile scattering feathers into space.
Behind them Grassmoor, shawled in cloud and distance.

Their cry speaks what a dropping stone might speak.
Bludgeoned all day to serve their tiny guts
or kick the wind for height; metallic, noisy,
scratchy, vulnerable, grabby, free—no words
will ever quite catch them. Holding a young
injured bird in fluttery hands is like
grasping the heart of a robot: it flails

in out of context, warm, dry as polystyrene,
feather and far-off eye wired God knows how
to a voltage of cells. Scarecrow or snowman
would be more human; yet these are the chosen
symbols of the poets. From Keats to Hardy's
geriatric thrush, from Hardy on to Yeats
(nightingales, skylarks, cuckoos, thrushes, swans)

they swarm like a new creation, needling
their single-minded mottoes on the heart.
Evolved from dinosaurs, scientists now say—
a metamorphosis to lift off the mind!
Vaulting clear out of Caliban's bone
and armour they leapt for the sustaining air,
but keep a grumpy claw in their demeanour.

Footnote

"I should have liked to produce a good book. This has not come about,
but the time is past in which I could improve it."
                  —Wittgenstein, Preface to *Philosophical Investigations*

Yes, yes, Ludwig. Locke under-laboured
for Newton, Shakespeare once fancied he
could write a play. You tip away
your thoughts as you tipped your sherry
slyly into the pub's potted palm. Miss
Anscombe was impressed; we're all impressed.
That camp bed in your rooms at Cambridge,
that modest card table, that screaming absence
of books and cultural clutter with which
the literati insulate their minds,
those monkish silences, migrating to
the wild nesting grounds of thought,
that intellectual amnesia (*viz.* Kant),
That Popeish look at Ryle, that declination
of all ancestry but God . . . Great men
have been among us: no vanity
like that of the great, who estimate
their value to a hairsbreadth ('Yeats,
Valéry and I . . .' the Possum was wont
to begin). We're grateful for the harvest,
amused to see you squirreling it away.
Whether to bombard us with kernels
or with shells; sit up and gnaw at truth
or bolt for the soaring ladder of your pride?

Images At Night

A cat with moonstruck eyes licking its paw;
old Tolstoy in a smock, implacable
as holy mother Russia; my youngest son
looking, did he but know it, like Napoleon;
'Arbre et Oiseaux, Hiver'—insouciant
young and spendthrift, I bought that in Villefranche
before the Flood; likewise this aboriginal
red abstract that bloodies one whole wall.
Treading the hours to a mulch, I drink
to all who taught the eyes to think,
the mind to mind its business. My belly boasts
no Mendelssohnian scamper past the post
just islands of hired chairs,
                              a few programme notes . . .

Strike up! I want to trawl for love again,
howl nightly at the rooftops; like old Leo's pen
pack all my limbs to horse, and rage
into the margin of another page.
Tomorrow, oh tomorrow I'll amass such tact
as boils the pigment on that red abstract.